9/11

P9-CME-885

RESCUING Animals FROM DISASTERS

SAVING ANIMALS AFTER FLOODS

by Joyce Markovics

Consultant: Dick Green, Ed.D.
ER Manager—Disasters
International Fund for Animal Welfare (IFAW)
World Headquarters
Yarmouth Port, Massachusetts

BEARPORT
PUBLISHING

New York, New York

Credits

Cover and Title Page, © Kham/Reuters/Landov and Joe Raedle/Getty Images; 4, © Steve Pope/EPA/Landov; 5T, © Molly Wald/Best Friends Animal Society; 5B, © Olson/Getty Images; 6, © John Stanmeyer/VII/Corbis; 7, © Win McNamee/ Getty Images; 8, © IFAW/Colleen Cullen; 9T, © IFAW/Colleen Cullen; 9B, © AP Photo/Sue Ogrocki; 10L, © Molly Wald/ Best Friends Animal Society; 10R, © American Humane Association; 11, Courtesy of Farm Sanctuary; 12L, © Cheri Deatsch/ Kinship Circle; 12R, Courtesy of Farm Sanctuary; 13L, Courtesy of Farm Sanctuary; 13R, Courtesy of Farm Sanctuary; 14, © IFAW/Deborah Gleason; 15T, © IFAW/Colleen Cullen; 15B, © American Humane Association; 16, © Frank Polich/Reuters/ Landov; 17, © Brandon Pollock/Waterloo Courier; 18, © AP Photo/Ajit Solanki; 19, © IFAW/Prayas; 20, © AP Photo/ Khalid Tanveer; 21, © Majid Hussain/Rex USA/BEImages; 22, © Newspix/Rex USA/BEImages; 23, © Nick de Villiers/AFP/ Getty Images/Newscom; 24, © Courtesy of Farm Sanctuary; 25, © Courtesy of Farm Sanctuary; 26, © Courtesy of Farm Sanctuary; 27, © Journal Newspaper Photo by Ron Agnir; 28, © Manuel Lopez/Reuters/Landov; 29, © Laszlo Balogh/ Reuters/Landov.

Publisher: Kenn Goin
Senior Editor: Lisa Wiseman
Creative Director: Spencer Brinker
Design: Dawn Beard Creative and Kim Jones
Photo Researcher: Daniella Nilva

Library of Congress Cataloging-in-Publication Data

Markovics, Joyce L.
  Saving animals after floods / by Joyce Markovics.
      p. cm. — (Rescuing animals from disasters)
  Includes bibliographical references and index.
  ISBN-13: 978-1-61772-292-9 (library binding)
  ISBN-10: 1-61772-292-8 (library binding)
  1. Animal rescue—Juvenile literature. 2. Floods—Juvenile literature. I. Title.
  QL83.2.M37 2012
  636.08'32—dc22

2011009354

Copyright © 2012 Bearport Publishing Company, Inc. All rights reserved. No part of this publication may be reproduced in whole or in part, stored in a retrieval system, or transmitted in any form or by any means, electronic, mechanical, photocopying, recording, or otherwise, without written permission from the publisher.

For more information, write to Bearport Publishing Company, Inc., 45 West 21st Street, Suite 3B, New York, New York 10010. Printed in the United States of America.

072011
042711CGF

10 9 8 7 6 5 4 3 2 1

CONTENTS

Water, Water Everywhere

The winter of 2007 brought nearly four feet (1.2 m) of snow to eastern Iowa. A few months later, spring rainstorms pounded the area. The melted snow along with the heavy rains filled nearby rivers, causing them to swell and overflow their **banks**. Even though wall-like structures called **levees** had been built near the river banks to stop overflows, there was just too much water. In June 2008, some of the levees failed, causing water to spill onto farmland and wash away roads and buildings.

Nine rivers overflowed their banks in Iowa in 2008.

Jeff Boyer, a pig farmer in Oakville, Iowa, was worried about how the animals on his farm would survive the flooding. As Jeff waded through the rising water to get to his barns, he knew that he had to do something to save the 3,500 pigs that were inside. Jeff tried to set them free by shooing the animals out of the barns, but the water outside frightened them. It was then that Jeff was faced with a heartbreaking decision: **evacuate** or stay with the pigs. He and his family made the painful decision to leave. "It was the hardest thing I've ever done," Jeff recalled.

In Oakville, many pigs were trapped inside barns when their owners left them to save their own lives.

Iowa has more pig farms than any other state.

"Little Pink Dots"

Five days after the flood, Jeff set out in a fishing boat to see what had happened to his pigs and farm. The boat zipped across what appeared to be a huge lake. However, it was not a lake. The water Jeff was moving through was actually thousands of acres of flooded cornfields. When Jeff reached his farm, he found most of it destroyed and **submerged** under several feet of water. Seeing no signs of life, Jeff was sure that all his pigs had drowned.

After the flood, over 17,000 acres (6,879 hectares) of farmland in Oakville, Iowa, was completely submerged, including dozens of pig farms. Many farmers used boats to see the destruction caused by the flood.

A few days later, Jeff got a surprising call. He was told that workers from an animal rescue group had spotted from their boat "little pink dots" along one of his barns. They counted between 250 and 300 pigs. When Jeff heard the news he said he was "just kind of **flabbergasted**."

To escape from the floodwater, many pigs found safety on the roofs of submerged homes and farm buildings.

With the help of a **barge** and crane, Jeff and some other farmers pulled out as many of the surviving pigs as they could from the floodwater. Unfortunately, many were too sick or injured to be saved and were later **euthanized**.

To the Rescue

Jeff Boyer's pigs were not the only ones in trouble. The floods had also **stranded** thousands of pigs from other farms. Fortunately, several animal rescue groups, including American Humane Association (AHA), Best Friends Animal Society, International Fund for Animal Welfare (IFAW), and Farm Sanctuary, had come to Oakville to find and care for animals stranded by the floods. The groups sent **veterinarians**, animal handlers, and other volunteers to form a 25-person rescue team. The groups also sent supplies, such as food, water, and medicine, for the animals.

Rescue workers head out to look for stranded pigs.

Iowa was not the only state affected by the floods in 2008. Other midwestern states were affected as well.

The rescue team used boats and **four-wheelers** to search for the pigs. They found most of the animals along levees and patches of dry ground. The pigs had reached these areas after swimming or floating, sometimes for miles. Unfortunately, their journey took them through floodwaters **contaminated** with fuel and other harmful chemicals that had been swept away from farms and homes. As a result, the pigs were in danger of getting sick and dying.

Animal rescuers transported food and other supplies to the stranded pigs on the levees. The pigs, many of which hadn't eaten for days, were fed mostly apples and Gatorade.

The rescue team worked 16 to 18 hours a day for about ten days to save almost every pig in Oakville that had survived the disaster.

A pig found wandering on a levee

Hog Roundup

Many of the pigs the rescue team found were scattered along a 20-mile-long (32-km-long) levee. Whenever a group of pigs was spotted, the animals were rounded up and placed in nearby holding pens, where they received food and water. Soon after, the animals were led to a **livestock trailer**. The team guided them up a ramp and inside the trailer using large plastic panels called hog boards. The team repeated this process until they caught nearly 70 pigs in the Oakville area.

A few of the pigs were very scared, which made them difficult to catch.

One of the pigs the team rescued was a mother pig with seven ten-day-old piglets. The fortunate piglets earned the name the Lucky Seven.

A rescuer uses a hog board to get a pig into the trailer.

Once aboard the trailer, the pigs were transported to a holding area in another part of Iowa. There they received emergency medical treatment for any serious injuries, such as cuts, broken bones, and sunburn. From the holding area, the pigs were driven to Farm Sanctuary's New York **shelter**.

Farm Sanctuary has shelters in California and New York. The Iowa pigs were taken to the shelter in Watkins Glen, New York.

Piggy Patients

Upon their arrival at Farm Sanctuary, the pigs received a complete health **evaluation** and medical care. Besides being exhausted and terrified, many had serious health problems. For example, some of the pigs were badly sunburned after living outside for several days without protection from the sun. The team treated the burns with **aloe** and soothing creams.

In some cases, the pigs' sunburn was so severe that their skin turned black and peeled.

Other pigs had leg or foot injuries as a result of trying to escape the floodwaters. For instance, one very large pig had hurt her leg. To help it heal, the team put the leg in a special sling to keep the pig from putting weight on it. A few of the other pigs had **pneumonia** from inhaling the dirty floodwaters and were given **antibiotics**. Some pigs were too sick to be helped and had to be euthanized.

Farm Sanctuary workers provide medical care to one of the rescued pigs.

Over 65 pigs were brought to Farm Sanctuary from Iowa. The ones with serious medical problems, such as severe pneumonia or infections, were sent to nearby Cornell University's veterinary hospital for further treatment.

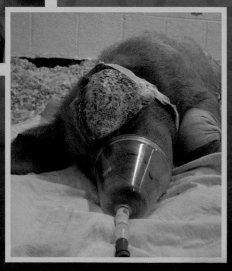

A pig being treated at Cornell University's veterinary hospital

Other Flood Survivors

Pigs in Oakville, Iowa, were not the only animals affected by the floods in 2008. Wildlife and pets in some of the surrounding states were also lost or stranded due to the flooding. For example, the U.S. Fish and Wildlife Service of Illinois helped rescue 20 tiny spotted baby deer, called fawns, near Quincy, Illinois. The young deer had been separated from their mothers during the flood.

This is one of the fawns that was rescued by the U.S. Fish and Wildlife Service of Illinois.

The fawns, less than a month old, had been found on dry patches of land and on a levee **overtopped** by water. The Fish and Wildlife Service team used large safety nets to capture the young animals. Then they moved them to a temporary shelter in Quincy, Illinois, which was built by the International Fund for Animal Welfare (IFAW) and the American Humane Association (AHA). There, the animals were checked for injuries.

A fawn being transported to the shelter

Along with the fawns, the shelter in Quincy, Illinois, housed about 6 cats, more than 12 dogs, several horses, chickens, and a pig.

A fawn is fed after being rescued.

Preparing Pets

Members of rescue organizations not only save wild animals, they also **reunite** rescued pets with their owners. Many times during the chaos of a **natural disaster**, such as a flood, pets and their owners become separated. Sometimes, when people have to evacuate an area quickly, they can't find their pets before they have to leave. So they rush out of their houses, just hoping that they will be back in a day or two.

A rescue worker carries a dog to safety during the flooding in Iowa.

All pets should have a collar, an ID tag, or a **microchip** that includes their owners' contact information. This can help rescuers quickly reunite pets with their owners after a natural disaster.

"You want to believe that your home is **invincible**," said Laura Bevan of the Humane Society of the United States. The reality, however, is that floods can destroy just about anything—even a house. It's best to be prepared with a plan of action before the next disaster hits. If it will not be possible to take the pets, there should be a plan to put them in a safe place, such as an animal shelter, before leaving.

These kittens are safe and sound at a shelter in Iowa after the floods.

Around the World

The United States is not the only country affected by floods. In 2006, floods swept across parts of India. The water destroyed villages and killed around 100,000 livestock, including cattle and donkeys. Members of the IFAW went out in boats and waded through the water to search for animals in trouble. The animals they found were given food, clean water, and medical care.

During the 2006 floods in India, water levels reached 10 to 20 feet (3 to 6 m) high in some areas.

The IFAW team passed out five tons (4,535 kg) of cattle feed, one ton (907 kg) of calf feed, one ton (907 kg) of grass and straw, and lots of dog biscuits to feed the hungry animals they found.

During the same disaster, IFAW also came to the rescue of a group of circus animals. Five elephants and three horses were found near the flooded area where they had performed. The rescuers led the animals on foot to a bridge—the only dry spot in the area. There the animals were fed fresh grass and were checked for injuries. Fortunately, most of them were healthy, except for one badly injured horse, which was treated on the spot by the team.

An IFAW worker provides fresh food to hungry circus elephants.

Saving Two Lives in Pakistan

Four years later, in 2010, floods devastated Pakistan, a country located next to India in southern Asia. While many people left behind pets and livestock when they evacuated their homes, others risked their lives to try to save their animals. For example, Jinda Mai, a 58-year-old woman, stayed behind with her buffalo instead of fleeing the disaster. "My buffalo is not a simple animal, she is my whole world," said Jinda. "She is my friend and I couldn't bear leaving her in floodwater."

People escaping the floodwaters in Pakistan in 2010

Jinda remained with her beloved companion for two days without food or fresh water. Fortunately, she and her buffalo were safely pulled out of the water near her flooded home and into a motorboat by government troops. They were extremely lucky to survive. Thousands of others were carried away and killed by the raging waters.

The country of Pakistan has a population of nearly 200 million people. The floods stranded millions of animals and people.

A man taking his livestock to higher ground to avoid the flooding in Pakistan

Flooded Down Under

More recently, in 2011, a huge area of Australia called Queensland was badly flooded. The floods affected the lives of millions of helpless animals. Ray Cole, who lived nearby, bravely offered a helping hand to one of the disaster's animal victims.

People walking through floodwater in Queensland

From on top of a bridge in a **suburb** called Ipswich, Ray spotted a young kangaroo, called a joey, drowning in a **torrent**. "I could just see its little head bobbing up and down and I knew it didn't stand a chance," he said. That's when Ray ran down to the water's edge and jumped in. He grabbed the kangaroo in neck-deep water and then swam to shore with the animal in his arms. Amazingly, the little kangaroo survived, and was adopted by a local family.

Ray Cole rescuing the young kangaroo

The 2011 Queensland floods have been described as the worst in the area in 100 years.

A Happy Pig-Tale

Thanks to the efforts of caring people, many animals that have survived floods have been given a second chance at life. A few weeks after the floods in Iowa, the pigs that were brought to Farm Sanctuary's New York shelter were thriving. Susie Coston, Farm Sanctuary's national shelter director, oversaw their ongoing health care. She also made sure they received lots of loving attention.

The Iowa pigs enjoying their very first New York snowfall

"To see how much the health of these pigs has improved since they were rescued from the floods is a **testament** to their will for survival. They swam for their lives and . . . they looked out for each other," said Susie.

Some of the Iowa pigs that were rescued from the floods were pregnant females. They gave birth to their piglets at the shelter in New York.

Susie Coston at Farm Sanctuary

Forever Homes

One of Susie's goals is to provide lifelong care or a loving home for each of the pigs that Farm Sanctuary saved during the 2008 floods in Iowa. Some of the pigs stayed at the shelter, where they now play an important role in educating children. Young visitors are taught how to feed and care for them, especially those that were injured in the floods.

A young visitor gives a pig a belly rub at Farm Sanctuary's New York shelter.

Other pigs that were rescued from the floods have been adopted by loving families or animal sanctuaries across the country. "We are so happy to be able to offer full lives to these animals. They certainly deserve it," Susie said.

These pigs have a second chance at life at their new home in West Virginia.

Some of the rescued pigs were placed in homes in Florida, Vermont, and West Virginia.

FAMOUS FLOODS AND RESCUES

Rescue workers have learned a lot from rescuing animals after floods. Here are two floods that put animals in danger.

Brazil, 2011

- In 2011, violent rainstorms caused flooding and **mudslides** that buried entire towns in southeast Brazil, killing nearly 1,000 people.
- When rescue workers reached some of the hard-hit areas, they found many dead or dying dogs, cats, and horses.
- The Animal Solidarity Campaign (SUIPA), a team of veterinarians, nurses, and volunteers, treated and cared for sick and injured animals.
- Some animal rescue groups set up shelters for lost or abandoned animals, with hopes that the pets' owners would come back for them.

Mexico, 2007

- After ten days of heavy rains in 2007, floods swept across the state of Tabasco in southern Mexico. The water rose nearly 15 feet (4 m) in some areas. More than a million people were affected.
- In the countryside, as many as 100,000 cattle were reported stranded by the floods. Some cattle were spotted huddled together on patches of high ground.
- Thousands of cats and dogs died in homes that were flooded.
- IFAW delivered food and medicine to hungry or sick animals throughout Tabasco.

A man swims with his dog through a flooded street in Mexico in 2007.

ANIMALS AT RISK FROM FLOODS

Floods are dangerous natural disasters that can affect different animals in different ways.

Pets

- Small pets, such as cats, dogs, rabbits, or birds, that are left behind in a home during a flood can drown, starve, or be poisoned by contaminated floodwaters.

- To protect themselves during a flood, cats usually hide in dark, hard-to-reach places. This makes them especially difficult for rescuers to find.

- Even pet fish need to be rescued from floods. That's because floodwaters are usually contaminated with waste and harmful chemicals, which can get into tanks and kill fish. Also, floodwaters are often very cold, and pet fish need warm water to survive.

Wildlife

- Large animals, such as deer, have an easier time escaping floods than smaller animals, such as mice and lizards, because they can move more easily to higher ground.

- Wild animals that live in **burrows** are at high risk of drowning during a flood. When their burrows fill with water, they have little chance to escape.

- Floodwaters can also wash away or submerge much of the food that wildlife needs to eat in order to survive.

Hundreds of deer walk through a flooded forest in Hungary

29

GLOSSARY

aloe (AL-oh) a plant whose juice is used to help heal burns and cuts

antibiotics (*an*-ti-bye-OT-iks) medicines that slow the growth of or kill bacteria

banks (BANGKS) the land along both sides of a river

barge (BARJ) a flat-bottomed boat used to carry goods

burrows (BUR-ohz) holes or tunnels in the ground made by animals to live in

contaminated (kuhn-TAM-uh-*nay*-tid) made dirty or unfit for use

euthanized (YOO-thuh-nized) having ended the life of a suffering animal in a humane way

evacuate (i-VAK-yoo-*ate*) to leave a dangerous area

evaluation (i-*val*-yoo-AY-shuhn) an idea that has been formed about something to help determine action

flabbergasted (FLAB-ur-*gass*-tid) stunned

four-wheelers (FOR-WEEL-urz) vehicles with four large wheels that are ridden like motorcycles and can travel over rough ground

invincible (in-VIN-suh-buhl) unable to be beaten or defeated

levees (LEV-eez) wall-like structures made of earth, concrete, or other material, built next to a body of water to prevent flooding

livestock (LIVE-*stok*) animals raised on a farm or a ranch, such as horses or sheep

microchip (MYE-kroh-*chip*) a tiny piece of electronic material in which identifying information is stored

mudslides (MUHD-slyedz) large amounts of mud or earth that move rapidly down a hill

natural disaster (NACH-ur-uhl duh-ZASS-tur) an event, such as a flood or an earthquake, that is caused by nature rather than people

overtopped (*oh*-vur-TOPT) having risen over the top of

pneumonia (noo-MOH-nyuh) a disease of the lungs that makes it difficult to breathe

reunite (ree-yoo-NITE) to come together again

shelter (SHEL-tur) a place where a person or animal is safe and protected

stranded (STRAND-id) left in a dangerous or unfamiliar place

submerged (suhb-MURJD) sunk beneath water

suburb (SUHB-urb) an area of homes and businesses close to a city

testament (TESS-tuh-muhnt) proof

torrent (TOR-uhnt) a violent, swiftly flowing stream of water

trailer (TRAYL-ur) a vehicle towed by a car or a truck that carries things or animals

veterinarians (*vet*-ur-uh-NER-ee-uhnz) doctors who take care of animals

BIBLIOGRAPHY

Brackett, Elizabeth. "Iowa Floods Wreak Havoc on Farming Communities."
PBS Newshour (June 20, 2008).
www.pbs.org/newshour/bb/weather/jan-june08/farmloss_06-20.html

Ryan, Kelly. "Queensland Flood: Cheers for Our Kangaroo Rescuer." *Herald
Sun* (January 13, 2011).
www.heraldsun.com.au/news/special-reports/queensland-floods-cheers-for-our-
kangaroo-rescuer/story-fn7kabp3-1225986668799

Farm Sanctuary:
www.farmsanctuary.org/mediacenter/2008/pr_pig_rescue_end08.html

Public Broadcasting Network:
www.pbs.org/newshour/infocus/floods.html

READ MORE

Fine, Jil. *Floods.* New York: Children's Press (2007).

Oxlade, Chris. *Floods in Action.* New York: Rosen Publishing Group (2009).

Woods, Michael and Mary B. *Floods.* Minneapolis: Lerner Publications
(2007).

LEARN MORE ONLINE

To learn more about saving animals after floods, visit
www.bearportpublishing.com/RescuingAnimalsfromDisasters

INDEX

ABOUT THE AUTHOR

Joyce Markovics is an editor, writer, and orchid collector. She encourages anyone looking for a pet to consider adopting one of the many homeless animals living in shelters across the United States.